Collins

The Secret Life
of Kittens

**David
Taylor**

First published in 2008 by Collins
an imprint of
HarperCollins Publishers
77-85 Fulham Palace Road
London W6 8JB

www.collins.co.uk

12 11 10 09 08
6 5 4 3 2 1

Photographs © Mark Read, except
p.35 © iStockphoto.com/Matthew Scherf
p.47 © iStockphoto.com/Patricia Edel
p.63 © iStockphoto.com/Davide Fiorenzo De Conti

A catalogue record for this book is available from the British Library.

Series Editor: Julia Thynne
Designer: Heike Schüssler

ISBN-13: 978-0-00-726360-8

Colour reproduction by Colourscan, Singapore
Printed and bound in Malaysia by Imago

Looking out
for lunch?

This two-week old kitten eagerly awaits the arrival of its mother and her milk supply. Soon it will be suckling and, like most kittens, purring with pleasure as it does so. The queen's milk contains almost twice the amount of fat and three times the protein of cow's milk, but less milk sugar. This nutritious liquid enables a kitten to double its birth weight of about 85 grams by the end of its first week of life.

I can see
clearly now

Kittens are born with their eyes closed and usually begin to open them at around five to ten days old. This two-week-old can now clearly see his mother and littermates. While his eyes were closed he found his way to her by the smell of the teat and by his highly developed sense of touch, picking up the vibrations caused by her purring in order to attract her brood to 'come and get it'!

Learning to play,
learning to hunt

This young tiger pounces on his prey – well, he thinks he's a tiger. Playing is much more than mere fun for young cats. It is a vital way of learning and enhancing the natural behavioural skills that have made them such a successful species. In the wild, cats spend up to six hours a day hunting. So in the home owners should provide an imaginative variety of toys and spend time each day playing with their pet.

Different coats
for different folks

This pair of rascals are from the same litter, so how can they look so very different? The answer is that each kitten develops from a separate ovum (egg) within which the genes controlling the coat features of the mother and father combine in a random manner at the moment of conception. Of course, identical twin kittens developing from the same egg will have similar coat features.

Uh-ho!
What was that?

If trouble is brewing, say the cross-eyed tom from next door comes a-lurking, the queen will suddenly growl an alarm call and instantly all her kittens will scatter and hide while she sorts the intruder out. They will remain motionless until the alarm is over. Cubs of wild species like the Bobcat act similarly when danger threatens. A Black-footed cat queen even emits a special 'all clear' call when the coast is clear.

The cat's whiskers

Kittens and adult cats gather important information from their surroundings via their whiskers. They serve as wind detectors, enabling the animal to pinpoint the direction from which any particular odour is coming. Loss of its whiskers will impair a kitten's sense of orientation in its surroundings, which is why a mother cat sometimes bites off the whiskers of kittens who tend to stray too far away!

Curiouser
and curiouser

This six-week-old kitten is likely to be developing the exploration bug. Everything he comes across must be investigated, tested and, if possible, played with. Now the owner must be vigilant in guarding the youngster against the many hazards that it may come across in the family home. Wires and cables must be kept hidden, fireguards put in place and washing-machine doors firmly closed. It is true that, sadly, curiosity can kill the cat.

Like mother,
like child

The average size of a litter is between three and five kittens. The largest litter where all kittens survived was 14, achieved by 'Bluebell', a Persian, in South Africa in 1974. To rear such a large bunch unaided would have been impossible for 'Bluebell' as she only had the usual eight teats, and kittens insist on monopolising the one particular teat from which they always suckle. But, luckily, her owners were able to lend a hand and bottle-feed half of the youngsters.

While the
dog's away

Accustomed to its mother's rich milk, a kitten may be hesitant when sampling water for the first time but, as soon as it moves on to eating some solid food, and for the rest of its life, water should always be available for the cat. Although saucers of milk have been associated with cats since time immemorial, cow's milk is not a natural drink for felines. Some individuals cannot tolerate it and develop milk sensitivity.

'Where's my dinner?'

'Digby' here is six weeks old and calling loudly to be fed. His mother still allows him to suckle but, in addition, he increasingly relishes the tinned 'human-type' baby food as well as mashed-up fillets of sardine – in oil or tomato sauce: he's not fussy – that his owner provides. Soon he should be moving on to some sort of proprietary kitten food.

A priceless puss

This rescue kitten is as beautiful as any cat on the planet and no less desirable than one of those feline aristocrats that pose and preen at pedigree cats shows. The world's most expensive kitten to date, a second generation Bengal, was sold for £25,000. But a rescue kitten can be obtained for a donation of your choice. If the kitten has been vaccinated and neutered, and you can afford it, I suggest you give around £50, to cover some of the rescue organisation's costs.

What is the
'milk tread'?

As the kittens start to feed contentedly from their mother, they begin the 'milk tread', making alternating pushing movements of their fore paws, pressing them against her breast as they suck. This gentle kneading stimulates the 'let down' of milk. Often the kittens purr softly as they tread. The 'milk tread' is also performed by the cubs of lions, tigers and other wild cats as well as by the young of otters, sea otters, foxes and badgers.

27

Watch with mother

This peeping tom is only a fortnight old but already he is learning a lot by watching, particularly watching his mother. Wild cubs and kittens learn to hunt by watching how Mum does it. Domestic kittens quickly learn how to press a lever to gain a food reward by copying their mother's actions. What is more, they learn faster watching their own mother than if the 'demonstrator' is an unrelated but friendly female.

'Look what I caught!'

Having watched their mother's hunting technique when out mousing in the garden or barn, kittens can't wait to have a go. Toy animals make perfect substitutes for real rodents and can just as easily be stalked, ambushed, pounced upon and despatched with a 'lethal' bite. These kittens may then grow up to be even better mousers than 'Mickey' of Burscough, Lancashire, who killed over 22,000 mice in 23 years.

'Who, and what, are you?'

For a cat to develop normally and become a happy member of feline (and human) society without fears, phobias and anti-social attitudes, it is important that it has the opportunity during its first months of life of socialising with human beings and other animals. Of course, if, as here, this involves it getting to know little furry creatures of other species, it would be prudent for owners to supervise things.

Now, where is my litter tray?

When kittens have begun eating solid food their mother, understandably, decides that her job of cleaning them up after they have passed water or a motion is over. It is now up to the owner to provide the youngsters with a small, shallow litter tray which is best placed close to the mother's larger tray. Most kittens quickly cotton on to using it. Any kitten that doesn't should be popped onto the tray as soon as it prepares to squat elsewhere.

Steer clear of
the cat's eyes

This nine-week-old kitten, 'Ziggy' has been vaccinated against the most important feline virus diseases for the first time, but cannot be allowed outside until he's had his second shot in three weeks time. For now he is happy stalking moths in the jungle that is his owner's conservatory. Like most cats he is particularly active at dawn and at dusk, key hunting times for cats of all kinds. Unfortunately for him, 'Ziggy' has yet to catch his first moth!

Learning
to talk 'cat'

Cats do have a language and kittens must learn how to talk 'cat'. To begin with the vocabulary of kittens is limited to a high-pitched, rather thin 'mew' – a plea for help and a louder more frantic 'MEW!' – help, please, a.s.a.p! They understand their mother's 'MEE-OW' (come and feed), meow (follow me), ME-RRROW, which is more of a sharp growl, (take cover!), mer-ROW! (stop that at once!) and a rather bubbly 'mreeeep' (a friendly greeting).

Here's a good
place for a nap

The 'milk tread' which a kitten associates with
the immensely pleasurable process of suckling
from its mother is carried on into later life.
Older kittens and adults continue to tread,
particularly on soft, yielding surfaces such as
cushions, duvets or, of course, your tummy.
Are they recalling their days of infancy or simply
checking whether this might be a good spot to
snuggle down?

The feline
family bond

Feline society is essentially a matriarchy based on cooperation between mothers, daughters, grandmothers, sisters and aunts. The strong bonds between siblings can last throughout their lives. Littermates make the best housemates, and if you want a multi-cat household, it is wisest to keep littermates together. Newcomer cats from outside the family can be introduced but only gradually and in a way not deemed to be threatening.

I may look cute,
but I'm dangerous!

A kitten out practising its hunting technique may seem harmless enough but, as it grows older and if it is allowed to roam, it can become a killer with considerable impact on wildlife in the vicinity. It has been estimated that rural free-ranging cats in just one American state, Wisconsin, kill around 39 million birds each year. Worldwide they may have been involved in the extinction of more bird species than any other cause, except habitat destruction.

Suckle and
sleep in peace

The kitty system of 'teat ownership' prevents squabbling over places at the queen's 'milk bar'. It also ensures that the whole litter can speedily settle down to suckle in peace at feeding time. A picture of utter contentment, this little pile of ginger mini-mogs dream on, snug in the warmth of each other's bodies, secure under the watchful eye of their mother and with their tiny stomachs pleasantly replete.

I caught
the catnip!

We all know that cats adore catnip. Smelling, rolling in it, or chewing it evokes obvious delight and playfulness in the animals. But a kitten's reaction to catnip is inherited. There seems to be a 'catnip gene' which 30% of kittens do not have, and, consequently, these individuals don't get turned on by the plant. Even those kittens that do possess the gene will not usually respond to catnip's charms until they are about six months old.

Tabby in
a tight corner

The familiar tabby markings of a cat's coat have come down from its wild ancestors in North Africa. The pattern acts as highly effective camouflage in the animal's natural surroundings. For kittens it is an aid in concealing them from larger mammalian and avian predators and it is invaluable to the adult cat lying in ambush when out hunting. Surprisingly, the totally different, dramatic striping of a tiger's coat also helps it hide in its normal habitat.

What goes up...

Cats like UP! I suppose their delight in looking down on the world goes with their general air of superiority. Kittens soon learn the joys of mountaineering around the family home. And, of course, one of their favourite practical jokes is getting stuck up trees. One truly amazing feline alpinist was the four-month-old domestic kitten that, in 1950, climbed unaided to the top of the mighty Matterhorn mountain. And no, it wasn't wearing boots or carrying oxygen.

Taking
a smelling test

The tiny nose pad and the paw pads of a kitten are especially touch-sensitive. The kitten investigates the texture, shape and size of an unfamiliar item by, at first, dabbing at it gently with a paw, the foreleg at full stretch, and then more firmly, before closing in on it to use its nose for both touching and smelling. A kitten's sense of smell is twice as powerful as a human being's and an adult cat's 14 times so!

The importance
of kitty cuddles

It is important for the animal's social development to accustom a kitten to being picked up, but this should not be overdone at each and every opportunity. Small children need to be supervised when encountering kittens in order to avoid inadvertent rough handling. When picking him up, slip one hand under his tummy and grasp his body gently but firmly while supporting his bottom with the other hand. Hold him close to you. Do not pick him up by his scruff.

Eat up,
little one...

A queen will usually bring food to her kittens
when they are around five weeks of age. She
will not bring it in the form of live prey until
they are about three months old, by which time
a kitten's prey-killing skills have matured but
they are still somewhat hesitant about
launching their first attack. Most owners prefer
to keep mother and kittens well supplied with
food to avoid dying prey being dragged in.
Nevertheless, even well-fed cats present such
'gifts' to the household on occasion!

Go on,
I dare you!

Kittens love to 'play-fight' and it starts at an early age both with littermates or with other non-related kittens. It is part of the process of them learning to be cats – fearless, multi-skilled, hunters. And it is also fun, with the kittens alternating roles as predator and prey. One will be the stalker for a little while and then change its role to that of the stalked. Another function of play-fighting is to begin establishing the social hierarchy or 'pecking order' among the cats of the household.

Exploring
the big, wide world

When is the right time for kittens to leave their mother? I think at nine weeks of age. Any sooner and they are still unprepared for the big, wide world out there; any later and they may well show signs of grieving for their Mum and littermates. Of course if, when it's time to leave, they go to a new home along with one of their siblings that is ideal. Four of my five Birmans are all related and the whole bunch (and I) are as happily settled as can be.

Rearing
a friendly feline

If, for any reason, it is necessary to hand-rear kittens it is essential that they are not kept in complete isolation from other cats, otherwise they may well develop psychological abnormalities, perhaps becoming anti-social, neurotic or aggressive. Rearing should therefore be carried out in the presence of other cats so that they can watch and learn moggy methods and manners like they would have done from their mother and siblings.

Habits of the
maternal moggy

As soon as she has given birth a queen is ready to care for her young, removing any foetal membranes and licking their fur dry. Prolonged contact with her kittens at this time forges a powerful maternal bond which is vital for successful rearing. The queen will, in fact, accept strange offspring if given them early enough, but after she has had some time to become familiar with them, her responses become directed towards her own brood and to them alone.

'Where's my mum?'

Like human babies kittens can get the attention of their mother by emitting a distress call, in their case a plaintive 'meow'! This call can, in cases where the mother has so far been inattentive, even neglectful, towards her offspring, trigger her latent maternal responses. If an owner feels that a post-natal queen is not carrying out her motherly duties, the situation can often be corrected by picking a kitten up and thereby causing it to yell for its mum!

Night, night.
Sleep tight...

It's no secret that cats like to nap! They sleep for 13 to 18 hours a day, mainly during daylight hours. Only bats and opossums sleep longer – for around 20 hours a day. Newborn kittens sleep most of the time when they are not suckling. This is a sensible arrangement by Mother Nature ensuring that kittens do not wander away from the nest or make sounds that might attract enemies while the queen is away. As they grow their sleeping hours gradually become like those of adults.

David Taylor

David Taylor is a highly respected veterinary surgeon. The founder of the International Zoo Veterinary Group, he travels the world treating a wide range of animals. He is the author of many petcare books and has presented and featured in several TV shows. He is the proud owner of five Birman cats.

Acknowledgements

The publishers would like to thank the staff and kittens of the Mayhew Animal Home (www.mayhewanimalhome.org, 0208 969 0178) and the Diana Brimblecombe Animal Rescue Centre (www.dbarc.org.uk, 0118 934 1122).